Advertising Fast track

Accelerate Your Success with Advertising Fast Track, The Ultimate Guide to Reaching Your Goals Quickly

Andy F. Leach

DEDICATION

To all those who have the courage to dream big and strive for success. May this book serve as a guide on your journey to personal growth and achievement.

ACKNOWLEDGEMENT

Acknowledgement: I would like to express my sincere gratitude to all those who have supported me in the creation of this book. Thank you to my family and friends for their unwavering encouragement and belief in my work. Additionally, I would like to thank my editor, designer, and publisher for their tireless efforts in bringing this book to fruition. Finally, I am grateful to the readers who have chosen to invest their time and attention in the pages of "Fast Track Your Life." Your support means more to me than words can express.

INTRODUCTION

Maria was running late for her important meeting and she had just 15 minutes to reach her office which was located at the other end of the city. She was anxious and frustrated as she was stuck in heavy traffic and her car didn't seem to be moving an inch. Suddenly, she saw a billboard advertising Fast Track, a new ride-sharing service that promised to get her to her destination in record time.

Without a second thought, Maria downloaded the app and requested a ride. Within seconds, a car arrived at her location and she got in. The driver was friendly and understanding, and he navigated the traffic with ease, taking shortcuts and using alternative routes to avoid the congestion.

Thanks to Fast Track, Maria arrived at her meeting on time and stress-free, impressing her boss with her punctuality and professionalism. From that moment on, she became a loyal user of the ride-sharing service and recommended it to everyone she knew.

The Fast Track team had truly delivered on their promise of providing a fast and reliable service, and they had made a customer for life in Maria.

In the fast-paced business world, it's all about staying ahead of the game. The competition is fierce, and failing to plan is planning to fail.

- **Accelerating your business with fast track** Accelerating your business with fast track is a powerful way to stay on top, achieve your goals quickly, and stay ahead of the competition. By adopting a fast track approach, you'll learn how to streamline your processes, optimize your resources, and make the most of your time and energy. This book will serve as a guide, offering step-by-step strategies to help you transform your business and achieve success at an accelerated pace. Whether you're an entrepreneur, small business owner, or corporate executive, this book has the tools and insights you need to navigate your path to success with ease. So let's jump on the advertisement fast track and take your business to the next level!

- **Why should I choose advertising fast track for my business?**

Advertising fast track is a great choice for marketing because it offers a dynamic and innovative environment that allows for creativity and growth. By staying up-to-date on trends and technology, utilizing effective time management, and communicating effectively, you can achieve great success in this industry. Advertising fast track also allows for the opportunity to work with a diverse range of clients and projects, making it an exciting and rewarding career choice. Additionally, with the growth of digital marketing and the increasing demand for innovative advertising campaigns, advertising fast track is a field with great potential for advancement and career growth.

- **How this book can transform your life**

Are you tired of feeling stuck, unfulfilled, and lacking direction in your life? Do you want to achieve your goals and reach your dreams, but don't know where to start or feel like you don't have enough time? Look no further than "Fast Track Your Life", the ultimate guide to transforming your life in record time.

This book offers a proven blueprint for success, providing practical steps and insights for achieving your goals and unlocking your full potential. With "Fast Track Your Life" as your guide, you can overcome the obstacles that are holding you back and create the life you truly want and deserve.

From setting achievable goals and creating action plans to cultivating a success-oriented mindset and overcoming limiting beliefs, this book covers all the essential steps to fast-track your success and fulfillment in life. Whether you're looking to advance your career, start your own business, improve your relationships, or simply live a happier and more meaningful life, "Fast Track Your Life" is the perfect tool to help you get there.

So what are you waiting for? Start reading "Fast Track Your Life" today and begin your journey towards a brighter future.

- **Practical techniques and insights for personal growth and success for marketing fast track**

Personal growth and success are two things that many people strive for in their lives in business. Whether it's advancing in their career, improving their relationships, or simply living a more fulfilling life, everyone wants to reach their full potential. However, achieving personal growth and success can be a daunting task without guidance and support.

That's where advertising fast Track comes in. This book is a comprehensive guide to practical techniques and insights for personal growth and success. It provides readers with the tools and knowledge they need to overcome obstacles and achieve their goals.

One of the keys to personal growth and success is self-awareness. This means understanding your strengths and weaknesses and identifying areas where you can improve in business skills. Advertising Fast Track offers a variety of exercises and techniques to help readers build self-awareness and develop a growth-oriented mindset.

Another important aspect of personal growth and success is goal-setting. Without clear goals, it's difficult to know what direction to take and what actions to take to achieve them. Advertising Fast Track provides readers with a step-by-step process for setting achievable goals, creating action plans, and tracking progress.

In addition to practical techniques, Advertising fast Track also provides valuable insights into personal growth and success. The book examines the role of mindset, motivation, and resilience in achieving success. It also explores the importance of networking, collaboration, and mentorship in building a successful career or business.

Overall, advertising Fast Track is a must-read for anyone looking to achieve personal growth and success. Whether you're just starting out on your journey or looking to take your life to the next level, this book has something to offer. With practical techniques and insightful guidance, "Fast Track Your Life" can help you unlock your full potential and create the life you truly want.

- **The power of reading and applying the insights of this book**

The power of reading and applying the insights in "Fast Track Your Life" cannot be overstated. This book provides readers with a wealth of knowledge and practical techniques for achieving personal growth and success. The information contained within its pages has the potential to transform the lives of those who read it and take action on its teachings.

Reading "Fast Track Your Life" is the first step towards unlocking your full potential. The book provides readers with valuable insights into goal-setting, self-awareness, and the importance of mindset. With this knowledge, readers can begin to identify their strengths and weaknesses, set achievable goals, and develop a growth-oriented mindset.

However, reading is just the first step. The true power of "Fast Track Your Life" lies in its ability to inspire action. The book provides readers with a variety of exercises and techniques for implementing its teachings in their daily lives. By taking action and applying the insights in the book, readers can start to see real results in their personal and professional lives.

The benefits of reading and applying the insights in "Fast Track Your Life" are many. By learning to set achievable goals and develop a growth-oriented mindset, readers can gain a sense of direction and purpose in their lives. They can start to achieve the success and fulfillment they desire, whether that's advancing in their career, starting their own business, or improving their relationships.

In addition to personal benefits, the insights in "Fast Track Your Life" can also have a positive impact on society as a whole. By empowering individuals to reach their full potential, the book can contribute to the creation of a more prosperous, innovative, and collaborative world.

In conclusion, the power of reading and applying the insights in "Fast Track Your Life" is immense. By taking action on the teachings within its pages, readers can achieve personal growth and success and make a positive impact on the world around them. So don't wait any longer - pick up a copy of "Fast Track Your Life" and start unlocking your full potential today.

PART 1

MINDSET FOR SUCCESS

The mindset of business is a crucial component of achieving success in the corporate world. Your mindset is the attitude, beliefs, and emotions you hold towards your business and the challenges you face. A strong and positive mindset can help you face uncertainty, overcome obstacles, and stay motivated in the face of difficulty.

One key aspect of the mindset of business is having a growth mindset. A growth mindset refers to the belief that skills and abilities can be developed and improved through hard work, effort, and perseverance. This mindset is essential in the business world, where constant learning and adaptation are critical to success. By adopting a growth mindset, entrepreneurs and business owners can approach challenges as opportunities for growth and develop the resilience necessary to thrive.

Another important aspect of the mindset of business is having a vision and clear goals. Without a clear vision and goals, it's easy to get bogged down in the day-to-day tasks of running a business and lose sight of the bigger picture. A strong vision and goals give you direction and focus, help you make informed decisions, and motivate you to keep pushing forward.

Finally, the mindset of business requires a willingness to take risks. Business is inherently risky, and the most successful entrepreneurs and business owners are often those who are willing to take calculated risks and step outside of their comfort zones. By embracing risk and learning from failure, you can develop the resilience, adaptability, and creativity necessary to succeed in the ever-changing business landscape.

The mindset of business is a critical factor in achieving success in the corporate world. By adopting a growth mindset, having clear goals and a vision, and embracing risk, you can develop the resilience and creativity necessary to overcome challenges and thrive in the face of uncertainty as seen below:

1) Motivational and determination

In the Marketing Fast Track, being motivated and determined is key to succeeding. This means having the drive to learn and adapt, and never giving up when faced with challenges. A motivated marketer is always looking to improve, while a determined marketer never lets failures bring them down. These qualities are critical to keeping up with the fast-paced industry and achieving success. Marketing Fast Track is a highly competitive field that requires individuals to be motivated and determined in order to succeed. To be successful in this field, one must have the drive to learn, adapt, and persevere through the challenges that are sure to come.

Motivation is the key to success in any endeavor, particularly in marketing. The ability to stay motivated and driven is essential to achieving any marketing goal. It helps individuals to stay focused on their objectives and overcome obstacles that may arise. A motivated marketer is always looking for ways to improve their skills, knowledge, and expertise. They are open to learning new techniques and strategies that will help them achieve their goals faster and more effectively.

Determination is equally important. It is the ability to persevere through any obstacle and not give up until the goal is achieved. Determination is often what separates successful marketers from those who fail. The determined individual never lets failures bring them down, but rather uses them as learning experiences to become better and stronger. They have a clear vision of where they want to be and will stop at nothing to achieve it.

In the Advertising Fast Track, motivation and determination are critical to achieving success. The industry moves rapidly, and it requires individuals to stay up-to-date with the latest trends and technologies. A marketer who is motivated and determined can navigate these challenges with ease and will succeed in this fast-paced and exciting field.

2) Overcoming fear and self sabotage

Overcoming fear and self-sabotage in the advertising fast track is critical for success. To achieve this, it is important to identify your fears and self-sabotaging tendencies, set clear goals, surround yourself with positive influences, and view mistakes as opportunities for growth. With these strategies, you can overcome obstacles and achieve success in this exciting industry Overcoming fear and avoiding self-sabotage are crucial for success in the advertising fast track. The industry can be full of uncertainties and challenges, and it is easy to become overwhelmed or lose sight of your goals. However, there are several strategies that can help you overcome fear and self-doubt.

First, it is important to acknowledge and confront your fears. Identify what is holding you back and make a conscious effort to address it. This could mean seeking mentorship, additional education or training, or trying new approaches that challenge your comfort zone.

Second, it is important to recognize the signs of self-sabotage. Sometimes, we unknowingly engage in behaviors that undermine our success. These may include negative self-talk, procrastination, or avoiding opportunities for growth. Combat these tendencies by setting clear goals, breaking them down into smaller steps, and holding yourself accountable.

Thirdly, surround yourself with positive influences and a supportive network. This may mean seeking out a community of like-minded individuals who understand the challenges of the advertising industry and can offer support and encouragement.

Lastly, do not be afraid to make mistakes. Failure is an essential part of the learning process, and successful individuals in the advertising fast track use their failures as opportunities to grow and refine their skills. Embrace challenges, learn from setbacks, and keep moving forward.

In summary, to overcome fear and self-sabotage in the advertising fast track, identify your fears, acknowledge self-sabotaging habits, set clear goals, surround yourself with a positive community, and learn from mistakes. With determination and persistence, you can achieve success in this fast-paced and exciting industry.

3) **Mental toughness**

Mental toughness is important in advertising. It means staying focused, determined, and resilient when facing challenges or pressure. To develop mental toughness, have a positive mindset, take care of your mental and physical health, stay calm in tough situations, take risks, and learn from failure. By doing these things, you can become mentally tougher and succeed in advertising!

Mental toughness is a crucial trait for those working in the fast-paced and competitive world of advertising. It refers to the ability to remain focused, determined, and resilient in the face of challenges, setbacks, and pressure.

To develop mental toughness, it is important to cultivate a positive and growth-oriented mindset. Focus on the opportunities that come with challenges rather than on the difficulties themselves. Embrace feedback and criticism as opportunities for growth, and keep pushing yourself to improve.

In addition, it is important to develop a routine that supports mental and physical well-being. This may include regular exercise, healthy eating habits, mindfulness meditation, and adequate sleep. When your body and mind are in good shape, you are better equipped to handle the stresses of the advertising fast track.

Another key aspect of mental toughness is the ability to stay calm and level-headed in high-pressure situations. This means being able to think clearly and make rational decisions, even when time is limited and the stakes are high. To develop this skill, practice mindfulness meditation or deep breathing techniques to help center your mind and reduce anxiety.

Finally, it is important to take calculated risks and embrace failure as an opportunity to learn and grow. Remember that those who take risks and are not afraid to fail are often the ones who achieve the greatest success in the advertising fast track.

In summary, mental toughness is a crucial trait for success in the advertising fast track. It involves cultivating a positive, growth-oriented mindset, developing a routine for mental and physical well-being, staying calm under pressure, and embracing risk and failure as opportunities for growth. By focusing on these areas, you can develop the mental toughness needed to thrive in this challenging and exciting industry!

PART 2

ACTION STEPS FOR SUCCESS

If you're looking to achieve success in the fast-paced and competitive world of advertising, having a clear plan of action is crucial. Action steps can help you stay organized, focused, and on track toward achieving your goals. In this context, action steps refer to specific tasks, milestones, or objectives that you can take to move your advertising career forward. By developing and executing action steps, you can gain an edge in the advertising fast track and position yourself for success. In the following text, I'll provide some helpful tips and strategies for developing effective action steps for success in advertising.

A) **Setting clear goals**

Here are some tips for setting clear goals on the advertising Fast track:

1. Identify your overall objective: What do you want to achieve in advertising? Do you want to become a creative director or launch your own agency? Having a clear objective in mind will help you set specific goals.

2. Break down your objective into smaller goals: What milestones do you need to achieve to reach your objective? Examples might include building a stronger network, gaining certain skills or certifications, or delivering successful campaigns.

3. Make your goals specific and measurable: "Get better at advertising" is not a specific goal. "Learn how to use Google Ads to increase conversions by 30%" is specific and measurable.

4. Identify obstacles and mitigation strategies: What challenges might you face in achieving your goals, and how will you overcome them? For example, you might need to work on your time management skills, or find a mentor who can guide you.

5. Set timelines: When do you want to achieve your goals? Consider breaking them down into shorter-term and longer-term goals and assign deadlines for each.

By setting clear goals in advertising, you can track your progress, measure success, and stay motivated on your journey to success in the fast-paced advertising industry.

B) Creating a strong action plan

Developing a strong action plan is crucial for success in the fast-paced advertising industry. Here are some steps you can take to create an effective action plan:

1. Identify your objectives: What do you want to achieve in advertising, and why? Be specific and break down your objectives into measurable goals.

2. Prioritize your goals: Determine which objectives are most important and what

needs to be done to achieve them. Focus on the goals that are most crucial to advancing your advertising career.

3. Develop a timeline: Determine the deadlines for reaching your objectives and goals. This will help you stay on track and avoid procrastination.

4. Create specific action items: Break down your goals into specific, actionable steps. Include a detailed description of each step, including what needs to be done, who is responsible, and when it should be completed.

5. Allocate resources: Determine the resources that you need to accomplish your goals, including time, personnel, and financial resources. Make sure that you have access to the resources you need to succeed.

6. Monitor and evaluate progress: Regularly monitor your progress and make adjustments as necessary. Celebrate your successes and learn from your mistakes.

By following these steps, you can create a strong action plan that will help you achieve your goals and succeed in the fast-paced advertising industry. Remember to stay focused, motivated, and resilient, and don't hesitate to seek out advice and guidance from mentors and colleagues along the way.

C) Increasing productivity

Certainly, here are some tips to help you increase your productivity and succeed in the fast-paced world of advertising:

1. Set clear goals and priorities: Prioritize your tasks based on their importance and set achievable goals for what you want to accomplish each day. By focusing on your

top priorities, you can make the most of your time and increase your productivity.

2. Optimize your workspace: Make sure your workspace is organized, comfortable, and conducive to productivity. Eliminate distractions such as unnecessary clutter or noisy surroundings to help you stay focused and on task.

3. Use technology to your advantage: Take advantage of technology to automate repetitive tasks, schedule reminders, and stay on top of deadlines. Use software and online tools like project management systems to help you manage your workload effectively.

4. Work smarter, not harder: Look for ways to streamline your work processes and reduce the time it takes to complete tasks. Delegate tasks where possible to free up time for more important priorities.

5. Take breaks and recharge: Working relentlessly without breaks can lead to burnout and reduced productivity. Take breaks and carve out time for relaxation and self-care activities to recharge your batteries, clear your mind, and boost your energy levels.

6. Build a support system: Surround yourself with supportive colleagues, mentors, and friends who understand the challenges of the advertising industry. Lean on them for support, advice, and encouragement when you need it most.

7. Continue learning and growing: Stay up-to-date with the latest industry trends, techniques, and best practices to maintain a competitive edge. Attend conferences, read relevant industry literature, and seek out opportunities for professional development.

By following these tips, you can increase your productivity, work more efficiently, and achieve success in the fast-paced advertising industry. Remember to stay focused, positive, and committed to your goals, and do not hesitate to seek out support and guidance when needed.

D) Building Relationships for Success

Building relationships is an essential part of success in the fast-paced world of advertising. By building strong relationships with clients, coworkers, and industry professionals, you can gain valuable insights, boost your credibility, and increase your chances of success. Here are some tips on how to build relationships for success on the advertising fast track:

1. Be reliable and consistent: Consistency and reliability are key to building trust and establishing a good reputation in the advertising industry. Make sure you meet

deadlines, follow through on commitments, and consistently deliver high-quality work to earn the trust and respect of your clients and colleagues.

2. Practice effective communication: Effective communication is an essential component of building successful relationships. Listen actively, show empathy, and communicate clearly to build strong relationships with clients and colleagues.

3. Cultivate a positive attitude: Positive attitude and energy can be contagious, and they can help you build strong relationships even in challenging situations. Maintain a positive outlook, seek out opportunities to praise and encourage others, and approach problems with a solutions-focused mindset.

4. Build a robust network: Building a robust professional network of colleagues,

mentors, and industry professionals can help you enrich your career, gain new insights, and navigate challenges. Attend industry conferences, events, and networking opportunities to build connections and expand your circle of contacts.

5. Show interest in others: Demonstrating a genuine interest in the challenges, needs, and goals of others can help you build strong and long-lasting relationships. Ask open-ended questions, listen actively, and look for opportunities to help others succeed.

6. Demonstrate your expertise: Demonstrating expertise and knowledge in the advertising industry can help you build credibility and earn the trust of clients and colleagues. Share your knowledge through thought leadership content, presentations, and mentoring

opportunities to showcase your skills and expertise in the field.

Building successful relationships is essential to success in the fast-paced world of advertising. By cultivating effective communication skills, building a robust network, and demonstrating expertise and knowledge in the field, you can build long-lasting relationships that help you succeed in your career. Remember to stay committed, positive, and persistent in your efforts to build relationships, and do not hesitate to seek out support and guidance from mentors and colleagues when needed.

E) Overcoming Roadblocks

Overcoming roadblocks is an essential part of success in the fast-paced world of advertising. In the face of constantly changing technologies, emerging trends, and competing priorities, it is important to develop strategies to overcome obstacles and reach your goals. Here are some tips on how to overcome roadblocks on the advertising fast track:

1. **Stay focused on your goals**: When faced with obstacles, it is important to stay focused on your goals and priorities. Refocus on your end game and make sure your actions are aligned with your long-term objectives.

2. **Be proactive**: Take a proactive approach to identifying and tackling obstacles before they become bigger problems. Think ahead and anticipate potential roadblocks so that you can develop strategies to address them before they arise.

3. **Develop resilience**: Developing resilience is important for overcoming roadblocks and staying motivated in the face of setbacks. Cultivate a positive mindset, seek opportunities for growth and development, and find ways to reframe challenges into opportunities.

4. **Embrace creativity**: Embrace creativity and innovation as a means of overcoming roadblocks. Think outside the box, experiment with new ideas and approaches, and seek out inspiration from diverse sources.

5. **Seek out support**: Seek out support from colleagues, mentors, and industry professionals when you face roadblocks. Don't be afraid to ask for help or advice from those who have more experience or expertise.

6. Practice adaptability: Practice adaptability to help you overcome roadblocks effectively. Be prepared to adjust your tactics as needed and to pivot to new opportunities when obstacles arise.

In conclusion, overcoming roadblocks is an integral part of achieving success in the fast-paced world of advertising. By staying focused on your goals, being proactive, developing resilience, embracing creativity, seeking support, and practicing adaptability, you can overcome challenges and achieve success in your career. Remember to stay positive, persistent, and committed to your goals, and do not hesitate to seek out support and guidance from mentors and colleagues when needed.

As you navigate through your career on the advertising fast track, be aware of the potential challenges and roadblocks that you may face. Take proactive measures to overcome these obstacles and above all, stay committed and persistent in everything you do. Aim to make a positive impact within the industry, and focus on continually improving your skills and strategies. With these tips and best practices, you'll be well on your way to achieving success in advertising.

PART 3

VISUALIZATION & AFFIRMATION

Visualization and affirmation are helpful techniques that you can use in advertising to visualize your goals and affirm your abilities. Here are some easy steps to follow:

1. Think about what you want to achieve in your advertising career.
2. Use positive affirmations. Repeat positive statements to yourself to reinforce your beliefs and abilities.
3. Visualize your success. Imagine yourself succeeding in your advertising career and achieving your goals in detail.
4. Practice regularly. Set aside time each day to visualize your success and repeat your affirmations.

5. Stay focused on your goals and use visualization and affirmation to help you stay motivated and on track.

6. Embrace challenges and use these techniques to help you stay positive and overcome obstacles.

By using these techniques regularly, you can increase your focus, motivation, and confidence as you work towards your advertising goals.

Visualization and affirmation are powerful tools that can help you achieve your goals in advertising. By visualizing your success and affirming your abilities, you can increase your motivation, focus, and confidence, which are essential qualities for success in this fast-paced industry. Below are some tips on how to use visualization and affirmation to achieve success in advertising:

1. Start with a clear vision: The first step in using visualization and affirmation to achieve

success in advertising is to have a clear vision of what you want to achieve. Visualize your goals in vivid detail, including the specific outcomes you want to achieve and the steps you will take to get there.

2. Use positive affirmations: Affirmations are positive statements that you repeat to yourself to reinforce your beliefs and abilities. Use positive affirmations to build your confidence and self-esteem, and to counteract any negative self-talk or limiting beliefs that may be holding you back.

3. Visualize your success: Visualization involves creating a mental image of yourself achieving your goals. Visualize yourself succeeding in your advertising career and achieving your goals in detail. Imagine the sights, sounds, and feelings associated with your success, and visualize yourself overcoming any obstacles or challenges that may arise.

4. Practice regularly: To get the most out of visualization and affirmation, practice regularly. Set aside time each day to visualize your success and repeat your affirmations. The more you practice, the more deeply ingrained these positive habits will become, and the more effective they will be at guiding you towards success.

5. Stay focused on your goals: As you work towards your goals, stay focused on your vision and use visualization and affirmation to help you stay motivated and on track. Use your affirmations to reinforce your belief in yourself and your abilities, and use visualization to stay focused on your goals and maintain a positive mindset.

6. Embrace challenges: As you work towards your goals in advertising, you will inevitably face challenges and obstacles. Use visualization and affirmation to help you stay positive and focused in the face of these challenges. Imagine yourself overcoming these obstacles and

achieving your goals despite any setbacks or difficulties.

In conclusion, visualization and affirmation are powerful tools that can help you achieve success on the advertising fast track. By visualizing your success, using positive affirmations, and staying focused on your goals, you can increase your motivation, focus, and confidence. Practice regularly, stay committed to your vision, and embrace challenges as opportunities.

PART 4

HABITS OF SUCCESS

1. Focus on clear goals: Set clear goals for what you want to achieve in your marketing career.

2. Create positive habits: Develop positive habits that will help you achieve your goals, such as setting daily priorities, staying organized, and staying up-to-date on industry trends.

3. Continuously learn: In order to stay on the fast track in marketing, it's important to stay informed about the latest trends, technologies, and best practices. Seek out opportunities to learn, such as attending conferences and seminars or taking online courses.

4. Communicate effectively: Successful marketers know how to communicate effectively with their colleagues and clients. Hone your communication skills through practice and by seeking feedback from others.

5. Embrace data: Data analysis is a crucial aspect of marketing success. Learn how to collect,

analyze, and interpret data to make informed decisions.

6. Stay adaptable: Marketing is an ever-changing field, so it's important to stay adaptable. Stay up-to-date on the latest technologies and best practices, and be willing to adapt your strategies when necessary.

By developing these habits for success, you can stay on the fast track in your marketing career and achieve your goals.

- **Replacing Bad Habits**

These are comprehensive guides on replacing bad habits with good ones on the advertising fast track:

1. **Identify your bad habits**: The first step to replacing bad habits with good ones is identifying the bad habits that are holding you back. Take a look at your work routine and identify any habits that may be hindering your productivity or success.

2. **Identify the triggers**: Once you've identified your bad habits, it's important to understand what triggers them. Triggers can be anything from stress to boredom to procrastination. This will help you develop strategies to avoid those triggers in the future.

3. **Make a plan**: Creating a plan is essential in replacing bad habits with good ones. Make a list of the new habits you want to adopt and identify specific actions you can take to make those habits stick.

4. **Start small**: Trying to overhaul your entire routine all at once can be overwhelming. Start by focusing on one or two habits at a time and gradually incorporating more as you see success.

5. **Hold yourself accountable**: Find ways to hold yourself accountable for your new habits. Share your goals with a colleague or friend, or use a habit tracking app to monitor your progress and hold yourself accountable.

6. **Celebrate your successes**: Celebrate your progress along the way. This can help keep you motivated and reinforce the positive changes you're making.

7. **Stay motivated**: Remember why you're making these changes and how they will help you succeed on the advertising fast track. Stay motivated by visualizing your success and keeping your goals in mind.

Here are some specific bad habits that may be hindering your advertising success and strategies for replacing them with good ones:

1. **Procrastination**:

Procrastination is one of the most common bad habits in advertising. To replace this habit with a good one, try breaking your work into smaller, more manageable tasks and setting deadlines for each one. Additionally, eliminate distractions and focus on the task at hand.

2. **Poor communication**: Poor communication can lead to misunderstandings and mistakes, which can undermine your advertising success. To replace this habit with a good one, practice active listening, be clear and concise when communicating, and ask for feedback to ensure understanding.

3. **Lack of organization**: Being disorganized can lead to missed deadlines and mistakes. To replace this habit with a good one, create a system for organizing your work, prioritize tasks, and make to-do lists to keep yourself on track.

4. **Negative mindset**: A negative mindset can sabotage your advertising success by making it difficult to stay motivated and see opportunities

- **Consistency and discipline**

1. **Set Clear Goals**: To achieve consistency and discipline in the advertising industry, it is essential to set clear goals. Setting goals will

allow you to develop a plan that will help you stay focused and motivated.

2. **Develop Consistent Habits**: Develop consistent habits that will help you achieve your goals. This includes setting a daily routine that includes activities that are relevant to your advertising work, such as checking industry publications for the latest trends, performing market research, or engaging with your peers.

3. **Stay Organized**: It's essential to maintain a high level of organization to avoid missing deadlines and making mistakes. Stay organized by developing a system for tracking your progress on tasks and keeping notes on important details.

4. **Prioritize Tasks**: Developing the habit of prioritizing tasks is essential in the advertising industry. Focus first on the most critical and time-sensitive tasks to ensure that you reach your goals within the specified time frame.

5) Avoid Procrastination: Procrastination can be one of the biggest obstacles to consistency and discipline in the advertising industry. Avoid procrastination by breaking tasks into smaller, manageable sub-tasks, scheduling time blocks for each task, and limiting your availability to distractions.

6. **Stay Focused**: Stay focused on your goals by avoiding distractions such as email notifications, social media feeds, and other non-essential tasks that can take your attention away from your advertising work.

7. **Monitor your Progress**: Monitor your progress by keeping track of your work and reviewing it regularly to ensure that you're meeting your goals, and making progress towards your objectives.

8. **Encourage Positive Habits**: Encourage positive habits by surrounding yourself with peers who share similar values, work ethic, and

ambition. This will help you stay motivated and on track in your advertising career.

In conclusion, developing consistency and discipline in the advertising fast track is imperative to achieving long-term success. By setting clear goals, developing consistent habits, staying organized, prioritizing tasks, avoiding procrastination, staying focused, monitoring your progress, and encouraging positive habits, you can maximize productivity, improve your work quality, meet deadlines, and achieve your goals as an advertising professional.

- **Time management**

Here's are some guide on how to manage time effectively in the fast-paced advertising market:

1. Prioritize Tasks: The advertising market can be fast-paced, and it's crucial to prioritize tasks to meet deadlines effectively. Start by listing all the tasks you need to complete and then determine which tasks are the most critical.

2. Use Time Management Tools: Time management tools like calendar apps, task lists, and project management software can help you stay organized and maintain a clear overview of your tasks.

3. Set Realistic Deadlines: Setting realistic deadlines is essential in time management. Break larger tasks into smaller ones and assign realistic deadlines to each sub-task.

4. Avoid Distractions: In the advertising market, distractions can hinder productivity, and it's important to avoid them. Turn off notifications or limit social media use during work hours.

5. Take Breaks: Taking regular breaks can help you reduce stress, prevent burnout, and boost productivity. Consider taking a short break every 90 minutes for optimal focus.

6. Delegate Tasks: Delegating tasks can help you free up time for more critical tasks. Work with a

team and delegate tasks to team members who have the necessary skills and expertise.

7. Set Boundaries: Setting boundaries is crucial to maintaining work-life balance. Determine your work hours and avoid working outside of those hours unless absolutely necessary.

8. Review and Adjust: Review your time management strategy regularly and make adjustments when necessary. Be willing to try new tools or approaches to find a system that works best for you.

In conclusion, time management is essential in the fast-paced advertising market. By prioritizing tasks, using time management tools, setting realistic deadlines, avoiding distractions, taking breaks, delegating tasks, setting boundaries, and reviewing and adjusting your strategy regularly, you can manage your time effectively and boost productivity in the advertising industry.

PART 5

COMMON MARKETING BLUNDERS EVEN INTELLIGENT INDIVIDUAL MAKE

Marketing is an essential aspect of any business, and while it may seem straightforward, there are several common blunders that even intelligent individuals make when it comes to marketing. These mistakes can range from misidentifying target audiences to poor messaging strategies, and they can have a significant impact on the success of a marketing campaign. In this article, we will explore some of the most common marketing blunders and discuss how businesses can avoid them to achieve their marketing goals.

1. Over complicating the message

One of the most common marketing mistakes is using overly complicated language or messages that fail to connect with customers. Marketers may be tempted to use complicated jargon or technical terms to make their products or services sound more impressive, but this often does more harm than good. Customers want to feel like they can easily understand what they are being offered, and if the language or message is overly complicated, they may become confused or disinterested.

Marketers may also use messaging that fails to connect with customers by focusing too much on features instead of benefits. Customers are much more interested in how a product or service can solve their problems or meet their needs, and if the message does not clearly communicate the benefits, they may not see the value in the offering.

Another mistake that marketers make is failing to consider the target audience when developing their messaging. Different demographics have different needs and interests, and a message that resonates with one group may not work for another. Marketers need to understand their audience's pain points, goals, and motivations to develop messaging that truly connects with them.

To avoid these common marketing mistakes, marketers need to focus on clear, concise language and messaging that clearly communicates the benefits of their products or services. They need to understand their audience and tailor their messaging to address their specific needs and interests. By developing messaging that truly connects with customers, marketers can build trust, establish credibility, and ultimately drive more sales and revenue for their business.

2. **Focusing on the products instead of the customers**

Focusing on the products instead of the customers is a common mistake that even intelligent marketers make. While it's important to have great products or services, it's equally important to understand who your customers are and what they want. Marketing efforts that focus solely on the features or specifications of a product often miss the mark when it comes to meeting the needs and desires of customers.

When marketers emphasize the features or specifications of a product, they risk alienating potential customers who don't understand or don't care about those details. Instead, they should focus on communicating the benefits of the product in a way that speaks directly to the needs and wants of the target audience. This helps potential customers to see how the product can help them solve a problem or achieve a goal.

To avoid this common mistake, intelligent marketers take the time to get to know their target audience. They research the demographic, lifestyle, and buying habits of their target customers to gain a deeper understanding of their motivations. They use this information to develop messaging and campaigns that highlight the benefits of their products or services in a way that resonates with their customers.

By focusing on the customer, rather than the product, marketers can build deeper connections with their target audience, establish trust and loyalty, and ultimately boost sales and revenue for their business. It's a simple shift in focus that can have a tremendous impact on the success of a marketing campaign.

Companies sometimes prioritize their products or services instead of understanding the desires of their target customers in an effort to differentiate themselves from their competitors. They believe that if they have a superior product or service, then customers will automatically be drawn to it. However, this is a misguided approach that can lead to missed opportunities and ultimately, decreased sales.

By not understanding their target customers, companies may fail to identify what their customers truly want or need, resulting in a product or service that does not meet those desires. Even if the product or service is of high quality, if it doesn't align with the needs and desires of the target audience, it will struggle to gain traction.

Furthermore, by prioritizing their product or service, companies may overlook important market trends, changing customer needs, and competitive pressures. This can lead to a situation where the product or service becomes irrelevant or outdated, making it difficult to retain existing customers or attract new ones.

To avoid this mistake, companies need to prioritize understanding their target customers. This means conducting market research, analyzing customer data, and gathering feedback through surveys and focus groups. By having a deep understanding of their target customers, companies can develop products and services that meet their needs, differentiate themselves from their competitors, and ultimately achieve success. Companies that prioritize their customers have a greater chance of building customer loyalty and earning repeat business, which is crucial for long-term growth and sustainability.

3) **Neglecting the power of storytelling**

Neglecting the power of storytelling is a common marketing blunder that even intelligent people make. While marketing is often thought of as a way to sell products or services, storytelling can be an effective way to connect with customers on a deeper level and build a brand's identity.

Storytelling allows companies to communicate their message and values in a way that resonates emotionally with customers. By presenting information in a narrative form, companies can capture the attention of their audience and create a sense of empathy and connection.

Unfortunately, many marketing campaigns fail to incorporate storytelling, instead opting for a dry and factual presentation of information. This can lead to customers feeling disconnected or disinterested in the product or service being offered.

Intelligent marketers understand that a good story can be a powerful tool in building a brand's identity and engaging with customers. They craft stories that are authentic, memorable, and meaningful, drawing on the values and history of the brand to create a sense of connection with their audience.

By neglecting the power of storytelling, companies are missing out on an opportunity to create a lasting impact with their marketing efforts. Effective storytelling can increase brand awareness, build customer loyalty, and even drive sales.

To avoid this common mistake, intelligent marketers prioritize storytelling as an integral part of their marketing strategy. By understanding the power of storytelling, they can create campaigns that truly resonate with customers and elevate their brand above the competition.

4) Failing to adapt to changing trends

Failing to adapt to changing trends is a common marketing blunder that even intelligent people make. Trends in technology, consumer behavior, and cultural shifts can all have a significant impact on a company's marketing efforts, and failure to keep up with these changes can often lead to lost opportunities and missed revenue.

One example of a trend that many companies have failed to adapt to is the rise of e-commerce. With more and more consumers shopping online, companies that rely solely on brick-and-mortar stores are missing out on a significant portion of the market. The same applies to mobile technology: companies that fail to optimize their marketing strategies for mobile platforms risk losing out on a vast audience of customers who prefer to use their phones for everything from shopping to communication.

Cultural trends must also be considered in marketing strategies. In recent years, consumers have become increasingly socially and politically aware, and companies that fail to connect with this trend may find themselves left behind. For instance, a well-intentioned ad that misses the mark in terms of cultural sensitivity can quickly become viral for the wrong reasons and damage a company's reputation.

Intelligent marketers stay on top of changing trends and adapt their strategies accordingly. They actively seek out new technologies and platforms to engage with customers, are attuned to evolving cultural trends, and are willing to take risks to stay ahead of the competition. They also analyze data regularly to monitor the effectiveness of their campaigns and make adjustments as needed.

To avoid the trap of failing to adapt to changing trends, marketers must stay informed and be open-minded to new opportunities. By remaining flexible and adaptable, they can create campaigns that resonate with their target audience and drive business growth. Ultimately, staying ahead of the curve and anticipating changes rather than reacting to them can mean the difference between success and failure in the constantly evolving world of marketing.

Marketing strategies must evolve over time to keep up with technology, social media, and customer behavior. In today's fast-paced digital age, it is no longer enough to rely on traditional marketing methods like print ads or TV commercials alone.

With the rise of social media platforms and the internet, customers now have more power and influence in the purchasing process. In order to reach and engage with these customers, companies need to be present where their customers are and must adapt their marketing strategies accordingly.

Technology is constantly changing and advancing, and companies need to stay up-to-date with the latest marketing tools and platforms to effectively reach their target audience. For instance, businesses can use artificial intelligence and machine learning to create personalized marketing campaigns and effectively reach their target audience across multiple channels and platforms.

Social media has transformed the way companies interact with customers and how customers perceive brands. Companies need to have a strong presence on various social media platforms and engage in two-way communication to build relationships with their customers. Social media monitoring tools can also help companies keep track of customer feedback and adapt their marketing strategies based on their customers' behavior and preferences.

Understanding customer behavior is also crucial for creating effective marketing strategies. Companies need to gather data on their target audience through methods such as surveys, focus groups, and online analytics. This data can help them develop personalized marketing messages and identify customer pain points that their products or services can solve.

In summary, to succeed in today's competitive marketplace, companies must adapt their marketing strategies to keep up with technology, social media, and customer behavior. By staying up-to-date with the latest marketing tools and platforms, engaging with customers on social media, and understanding the customer journey, companies can create effective marketing campaigns that resonate with their target audience and drive business growth.

5) Ignoring customers feedback

Ignoring customer feedback is a common blunder that even intelligent marketers can make. Customer feedback can provide valuable insights into how a company is perceived by its target audience and can help inform future marketing strategies and product development.

Some companies may be hesitant to collect customer feedback because they fear negative comments or may feel that the opinions of a few individuals are not representative of the wider market. However, ignoring this feedback entirely can be a costly mistake.

One of the biggest benefits of customer feedback is that it helps companies understand how their products or services are perceived by their target audience. This includes not only identifying areas for improvement but also recognizing what is already working well, which can be leveraged in marketing campaigns.

Additionally, customer feedback can help companies stay ahead of the competition by identifying emerging trends and unmet needs in the market. This can inform the development of new products and services or lead to improvements in existing offerings.

Intelligent marketers understand the importance of collecting customer feedback and actively seek out ways to do so. They may use surveys, focus groups, or social media monitoring software to gather feedback and analyze the results. They also take the time to respond to customer feedback, whether it is positive or negative, to show customers that their opinions are valued and to build a sense of trust and loyalty.

In summary, ignoring customer feedback can be a costly mistake for companies looking to stay competitive and grow their business. Intelligent marketers recognize the value of feedback and take the necessary steps to collect and analyze this information to inform their marketing strategies and drive success.

6) Replying too heavily on data

Relying too heavily on data is a common blunder that even intelligent marketers can make. While data can provide valuable insights into consumer behavior and the success of marketing campaigns, it is important not to lose sight of the bigger picture and rely solely on data-driven decisions.

One of the risks of relying too heavily on data is that it can lead to a focus on short-term results at the expense of long-term goals. While data can help optimize immediate marketing efforts, this approach may not necessarily be best for the overall health of the company.

Another potential issue with relying only on data is that it does not capture the full range of human motivations and emotions that drive consumer behavior. By focusing exclusively on what the data shows, marketers may miss out on important nuances or fail to recognize the impact of unquantifiable factors such as brand equity or emotional resonance.

Intelligent marketers strike a balance between data-driven decision-making and a more holistic approach that takes into account larger trends and consumer behavior outside of the data. By combining a deep understanding of target audience's needs and desires with analysis of data, they develop marketing strategies that are both informed by data insights and responsive to the broader context.

Overall, data should be seen as an important tool in the marketer's toolkit—not as a substitute for careful analysis and strategic thinking. Intelligent marketers recognize the value of data-driven insights but also understand the limits of what it can tell us and the importance of taking a wider perspective to drive business success.

In addition, Data can be extremely useful for making marketing decisions. By analyzing consumer behavior, market trends, and campaign metrics, marketers can make informed decisions to optimize and personalize their campaigns.

However, relying too heavily on data can lead to a lack of creativity and innovation, as marketers may become overly focused on what the data tells them to do, rather than thinking outside the box. This can result in campaigns that are formulaic and fail to capture the attention and interest of consumers.

Additionally, data can only provide insights into what has worked in the past, and may not necessarily be predictive of what will work in the future. This means that relying too heavily on data can also lead to missed opportunities or failure to adapt to changing market dynamics.

To avoid this pitfall, intelligent marketers strike a balance between data-driven decision-making and a more exploratory, creative approach. They use data to inform, but not dictate, their marketing strategies, and also prioritize testing, experimentation, and risk-taking to drive innovation and find new ways to connect with consumers.

At the end of the day, data can be a valuable tool in the marketer's toolkit, but it is important not to rely on it exclusively. By combining data insights with creative, strategic thinking, marketers can develop campaigns that are both effective and innovative, driving business success over the long term.

In conclusion,

Common marketing blunders include relying too heavily on data, neglecting the target audience, failing to differentiate from competitors, and poor communication. To avoid these, marketers should strike a balance between data-driven decisions and a more exploratory, creative approach. They should also prioritize understanding their target audience's needs and desires, conducting thorough competitor analysis, and ensuring clear and effective communication with their audience. Additionally, staying agile and adaptable to changing market dynamics can help prevent costly missteps. By avoiding these blunders and following these tips, marketers can develop effective campaigns that resonate with consumers and drive business succe

GENERAL CONCLUSION

- **Making advertising fast track a lifestyle**

To make advertising fast track a lifestyle, there are several steps you can take:

1. Develop Strong Work Habits: To make advertising fast track a lifestyle, you need to develop strong work habits that will help you stay productive and focused. This includes creating a daily routine that includes time for market research, client meetings, and creative work.

2. Stay Up-to-Date on Trends: Staying up-to-date on trends in the advertising industry is crucial for success. Make sure to read industry publications regularly, attend industry events and conferences, and network with your peers.

3. Be Creative: Creativity is the hallmark of the advertising industry, and it's important to cultivate a creative mindset. Make time for

brainstorming and idea generation, and constantly challenge yourself to come up with new and innovative concepts.

4. Practice Consistency: Practicing consistency is essential in the advertising industry. Make sure to stick to deadlines, develop a reliable work routine, and establish regular check-ins with clients to ensure that everyone is on the same page and that projects are progressing as planned.

5. Communicate Effectively: Effective communication is key to success in advertising. Make sure to communicate regularly and clearly with clients, colleagues, and other stakeholders to ensure that everyone is on the same page.

6. Be Passionate: Passion is critical for success in the advertising industry. Finding your passion and using it to fuel your work can help you stay motivated and achieve great results.

7. Stay Organized: Staying organized is crucial in the advertising industry, where deadlines, budgets, and other factors can quickly become overwhelming. Develop a system for tracking your tasks and projects, and make use of tools such as project management software, time tracking apps, and digital calendars.

By following these steps, you can make advertising fast track a lifestyle and achieve great success in the industry. It takes effort and dedication, but the rewards of a thriving advertising career make it all worthwhile.

- **Celebrating your success with Fast track**

Celebrating your business's success is an important part of inspiring and motivating your team, as well as showcasing the achievements of your business to the world. Advertising fast track offers a great way to promote your business's success and inspire employees and customers alike. With the right advertising campaign, you can share your business's milestones, awards, and accomplishments with a wider audience, while also increasing brand recognition and loyalty. You can celebrate success with an eye-catching ad that highlights your achievements or distribute a press release to industry publications to showcase your business's excellence. By celebrating your success with advertising fast track, you can create a positive image for your business while also motivating your team to continue striving towards excellence.

In conclusion, advertising fast track is a dynamic and innovative industry that requires a combination of skills, creativity, and effective time management. To thrive in this industry, it is important to stay up-to-date on trends, develop strong work habits, communicate effectively, and cultivate a passion for your work. By practicing consistency, organization, and creativity, you can make advertising fast track a lifestyle and achieve great success in the industry. With the right mindset and skills, you can shape the future of advertising/market and make a positive impact on the lives of your clients and audience.

www.ingramcontent.com/pod-product-compliance
Lightning Source LLC
Chambersburg PA
CBHW062239290526
45794CB00006B/2342